*Jim Larkin and the
Great Dublin Lockout of 1913*

John Newsinger

About the author

John Newsinger is Professor of History at Bath Spa University. His most recent books include *Orwell's Politics* (Macmillan, 2000), *United Irishman* (Merlin, 2001), *Rebel City: Larkin, Connolly and the Dublin Labour Movement* (Merlin, 2004), *The Blood Never Dried: A People's History of the British Empire* (Bookmarks, 2006) and *Fighting Back: The American Working Class in the 1930s* (Bookmarks, 2012).

Jim Larkin and the
Great Dublin Lockout of 1913

John Newsinger

Jim Larkin and the Great Dublin Lockout of 1913
John Newsinger
Published in July 2013 by Bookmarks Publications
c/o 1 Bloomsbury Street, London WC1B 3QE
© Bookmarks Publications
Cover design by Ben Windsor
Typeset by Bookmarks Publications
Printed by The Russell Press
ISBN 978 1 909026 37 7

Contents

Acknowledgements

Thanks to Kevin Devine and Martin Empson for helpful comments on the first draft and to Sally Campbell, Peter Robinson, Ben Windsor and Mary Phillips for their work on production.

Introduction

The Dublin Lockout of 1913 is without doubt the most important industrial struggle in Irish history. It was fought to determine who should be the dominant force in Home Rule Ireland—the labour movement or the employers. It was a concerted attempt with the backing of government, politicians, priests, the press, the police and the courts to crush militant trade unionism, in the shape of the Irish Transport and General Workers Union (ITGWU) led by Jim Larkin, once and for all. With incredible courage and in the face of great hardship, the Dublin workers held out for nearly six months. Solidarity was the watchword. Workers with the lowest wages and the worst living conditions in Western Europe, many of them casual labourers, at the mercy of their employers, joined together to fight the employers to a standstill. With overwhelming odds against them, the workers held on. And, it has to be insisted, the dispute could have been won.

The Lockout was also one of the most important industrial struggles in British history. It was part of the great wave of working class revolt that swept over the British Isles in the years from 1910 to the outbreak of war in 1914. The Lockout had tremendous repercussions in Britain as well as in Ireland. A victory for the Dublin workers would have shaken employers throughout Britain, while the defeat of the Dublin workers only gave them encouragement. The fight for solidarity with the Dublin workers was to be carried right into the heart of the British labour movement and served to lay bare the nature of trade union officialdom that was prepared to watch them go down to defeat in isolation.

The British union leaders were more concerned with defeating the rank and file challenge to their own position than they were with rallying to the side of the ITGWU in its battle with the Dublin employers. The weakness of the left in Britain was brutally demonstrated by its failure to wrest the initiative from the union officials, a failure that snatched away the prospect of victory and was to doom the Dublin workers to defeat. The failure of the largest Marxist organisation in Britain, the British Socialist Party, in this respect, provides an object lesson in how not to fight the class war. The dispute could and should have been won. If the British unions had blacked Dublin traffic in December 1913, if the rank and file had been well enough organised to take action independently and thereby force the TUC to fight, there is every reason to believe that the employers would have crumbled in the face of such an escalation of the dispute with many of them breaking ranks to settle on the union's terms. This was not to be.

Clearly, the experience of the Dublin Lockout and its ramifications in Britain has many lessons for the left today. It provides a tremendous and inspiring example of militancy and solidarity. The stand taken by the Dublin workers, steadfastly resisting an unprecedented employers' offensive for six months, against all the odds, and coming close to victory, is something we can all learn from. Similarly, the solidarity movement in Britain, spearheaded by the *Daily Herald*, then a radical fighting newspaper,[1] is an inspiration. But in the end, in order to protect themselves from their own rank and file, the British trade union leadership, cheered on by the leaders of the Labour Party, took steps to isolate the Dublin workers, preferring defeat to struggle. The left was not strong enough to prevent this betrayal. This is certainly a lesson we are still learning to our cost.

Today, a hundred years after the Great Lockout, in the middle of a sustained attack on the working class across the whole of Europe, and with the most right wing post-1945 government in power in Britain, is a good time to revisit the struggles of 1913, to recover something of the remarkable movement of working class revolt and resistance that went under the name of "Larkinism".

Chapter 1

Larkin: the early years

Jim Larkin remains a controversial figure—even his date and place of birth are contested: 1874 or 1876 for his year of birth and Newry (favoured by his family) or Liverpool as the place. Whatever the facts regarding his birth, he was certainly brought up in Liverpool, the son of poor Irish parents. He knew all there was to know about poverty and hardship from personal experience. He went out to work at the age of 11, after the death of his father. After a variety of jobs, in the late 1890s, he went to work on the docks. By this time he was already an active socialist, having joined the Independent Labour Party (ILP) a few years earlier. He was already well known as a public speaker, advocating the introduction of a democratic socialist commonwealth. Like many on the left at the time, he had little regard for trade unionism, considering the unions as the accomplices of capitalism and strikes as counter-productive, hurting the workers more than the capitalist. The way forward was via the ballot box and anything else was a diversion. Only in 1901 did he finally join the National Union of Dock Labourers (NUDL), influenced by Keir Hardie, who was urging that the unions should be won over to ILP social-ism. He was not a union militant, however, and by 1903 had actually been promoted to foreman at T&J Harrisons. This changed in June 1905, when 800 union members walked out on strike in an attempy to impose the closed shop. Larkin became one of the strike leaders. The strike was defeated when the Shipping Federation provided the firm with scabs. After 13 weeks the company withdrew union recognition altogether and only took back those workers it wanted. Larkin was not among them.

What this bitter, hard-fought dispute taught him was the need for organisation and solidarity on the job and the consequences when it was lacking. The strike at Harrisons transformed him from a woolly ballot-box socialist into an aggressive trade union organiser who was to preach the virtues of industrial militancy and class solidarity to considerable effect. For Larkin, the union rather than the ballot box became the instrument of social transformation.

He was taken on as an organiser by the NUDL, working in the ports of Scotland and Ireland. While his militant methods were certainly popular with the rank and file, they soon brought him into conflict with the NUDL leadership, in particular its general secretary, James Sexton. Larkin's most famous success was in Belfast in 1907 when he succeeded in uniting Protestant and Catholic workers against the employers. He brought the dockers out on strike and foiled the employers' hopes of breaking the strike with scabs by persuading the carters to refuse to cross picket lines. Even if the employers could unload the ships, they could not get the goods off the docks. The carters were locked out in reprisal. The dispute saw scenes of unprecedented working class unity on the streets of Belfast. When attempts were made to move goods off the docks, hundreds of Protestant shipyard workers reinforced the mainly Catholic picket lines and battled it out with the police. In the middle of July the police, who had their own grievances, mutinied and refused to continue providing escorts for the scab drivers. Troops were sent in and, in fierce clashes on 12 August, shot two men dead on the Falls Road.

Victory in the dispute was snatched away by the intervention of James Sexton, who was more concerned with quelling militancy than with actually winning. The carters were persuaded to return to work with a pay rise but no union recognition, leaving the dockers isolated and doomed to defeat. Whereas Larkin had preached unity, Sexton practised division. As far as Sexton was concerned the way forward for the trade union movement was to win the employers over by curbing militancy and showing how responsible they were. Coincidentally, in Sexton's case this was also the way to a safe Labour seat in the Commons, a knighthood and the personal friendship of leading Tory politicians such as Stanley Baldwin. As for Larkin, never again would he allow a dispute to be sold out from under him.

This phenomenon of the full-time union official being more concerned with establishing a good relationship with the employer than with winning the demands of the rank and file has a long history. One of the earliest attempts to theorise it was by the Fabian socialists Sidney and Beatrice Webb in their *The History of Trade Unionism*, first published in 1894 and soon after translated into Russian by Lenin and his wife, Nadezhda Krupskaya. What the Webbs pointed to was the emergence of a trade union civil service of full-time officials that was no longer of the working class, but instead acted as an intermediary between the working class and the employers. These officials developed their own corporate identity, their own distinct loyalties and interests that were best served by good relations with the employers. These relations might well be put at risk by rank and file militancy. Indeed the union itself might be put at risk if its members were not kept under control. They no longer worked on the job, experiencing life as their members experienced it. Instead in their new position as intermediaries they found all sorts of opportunities opening up for them. For a select few the House of Lords beckoned! Of course, it is important to remember that not all officials were the same; there were officials who would never fight, officials who would fight if they had to and officials who recognised that building the union actually required taking on the employers. They were all under the same pressures, however, and experience shows that even "left" officials, unless under the control of the rank and file, would succumb to the need for "compromise", for "responsibility" and for "moderation".[2] Larkin had plenty of experience of these concerns undermining militancy and snatching defeat from the jaws of victory.

Even while the Belfast dispute continued, Larkin was still busy organising elsewhere and by the end of 1908 had established NUDL branches in every major port in Ireland. Towards the end of the year, he fought and won a major carters' strike in Dublin, completely ignoring the NUDL head office. By now, however, the union executive was preparing to get rid of him. On 8 December 1908 he was suspended from his organiser's post. Together with activists and sympathisers from all over Ireland, Larkin issued the call for the establishment of a new Irish trade union to organise transport and general workers. A meeting of delegates took place in Dublin on 28 December and the Irish Transport and General Workers Union (ITGWU) came into existence on 4 January 1909.[3]

Chapter 2

Organising the union

The ITGWU was, in essence, a rank and file revolt against an entrenched NUDL leadership that refused to back its Irish members in struggle. Sexton was more interested in collaborating with the employers than in fighting them and this made a break with Larkin inevitable. At this time the rank and file dimension to the breakaway was arguably more important than its nationalism. Larkin's great strength as a union leader was always the way he maintained a rapport with the union membership. He was more of a rank and file leader, an apostle of militancy, than he was an official.

Hardly had the new union been established than it was embroiled in a bitter dispute in Cork where the local Employers Federation attempted to crush it out of existence. In June 1909 ITGWU members were locked out and the federation announced the introduction of a blacklist to ensure that anyone sacked for his union activity "shall not be employed by any member of the federation".[4] There were serious clashes between ITGWU members and the police and scabs. The Cork organiser, James Fearon, established a workers' militia, which Larkin later described as a precursor to the Irish Citizen Army that was to be established in 1913 during the Dublin Lockout. The dispute ended in defeat, with Fearon sentenced to six months hard labour following a pitched battle with strike-breakers. Soon after the defeat Larkin was arrested and charged with conspiracy to defraud, a charge got up by the Cork Employers Federation with the assistance of the NUDL leadership. At the end of 1908 Larkin had transferred funds from the Cork branch of the NUDL to help fight a strike in Dublin and was now charged with defrauding the Cork membership on the grounds that the Cork branch had not been officially recognised by the NUDL and that the money was used for unauthorised purposes. Sexton appeared as a key witness for the prosecution and played a crucial role in securing a conviction. In June 1911 Larkin was found guilty and sentenced to 12 months in prison. This was a clearly punitive sentence for what was really only a technical offence. There was no suggestion that Larkin had lined his own pockets; the money was used to help fight the Dublin employers. Indeed, it seems pretty clear that the severity of the sentence was intended to destroy both Larkin and the infant ITGWU. In the event, the ploy backfired. There was a campaign to secure his release and he was freed after only three months. On his release on 10 October 1910 a huge torchlight procession marched through Dublin to celebrate his return. The ITGWU had survived the attempt to strangle it at birth.

The ITGWU's drive to organise Ireland's unskilled workers into "One Big Union" has to be seen as part of the wave of working class revolt, the Great Unrest, that swept over Britain and Ireland in the period from 1910 until 1914. According to Bob Holton, this explosion marked:

> an important phase in the development of social relations between capital and labour. The two most immediate characteristics of the unrest were mass strikes and rapid trade union recruitment. From 1910 until the outbreak of war, working days lost rose to an annual total of 10 million or more, while trade union membership increased from 2.1 million to 4.1 million.

What was "most striking" about this explosion "was the high degree of aggressive, sometimes violent and often unofficial industrial militancy".[5]

The reality was that the revolt was not just against the employers but against the dead hand of the trade union bureaucracy as well. It showed a contemptuous disregard for procedures and agreements. The militancy and violence that were its hallmarks were absolutely necessary if victory was to be achieved. The only way the employers' resistance to union organisation could be overcome was by militant aggressive action accompanied where necessary by demonstrative violence. Scabs had to be shown that their strike-breaking would not be tolerated, especially not when the very existence of the union was at stake. The fact that unskilled workers were by and large unorganised was not some sort of natural phenomenon or a result of the "immaturity" of the labour movement. On the contrary, it was due to the way that the employers had defeated earlier attempts at organisation by strike-breaking, victimisation and blacklisting. Larkin, of course, had personal experience of this. The methods of respectability and moderation championed by the official union leadership had failed and they were swept aside. In their place, fuelled by anger and bitterness at years of mistreatment, was put unbridled militancy: the employers had to be battered into submission, and this could not be done politely, according to the rule book or without being prepared to break the law.

1911 was the year that the ITGWU securely established itself, growing from some 5,000 members at the start of the year to 18,000 at the end. That year saw a wave of militancy engulf both Britain and Ireland. In Britain between June and September "insurgent, largely unofficial, and often violent action was felt in all the major ports and on the railway system".[6] The ITGWU enthusiastically supported the strikes in Britain and its members in Irish ports refused to touch "tainted goods"—merchandise handled by scabs. The union actually paid strike pay (some £470 a week in total) to Irish seamen, members of the British National Sailors' and

Firemen's Union, in a gesture of solidarity. Inevitably, its own members were swept up in the dispute. In an editorial that appeared in the *Irish Worker* on 15 July, Larkin called on British workers to establish one Transport Union ("the time is rotten ripe"). As for the ITGWU, it was "national in name: international in name and object", committed to "the overthrow of the present brutal system of master and slave". This was not just empty words, because "we of the Irish Transport Union took our fate in both hands and refused to load or unload boats sailed or loaded by scabs. For our action we now have over a thousand men in dispute." Troops in Liverpool opened fire on a crowd attempting to free strikers being transported to Walton prison on 15 August, and they shot two men dead, Michael Prendergast and John Sutcliffe. Larkin condemned the shootings as "Murder Most Foul" in an editorial in the *Irish Worker*.[7] He knew both men personally from his Liverpool years. The ITGWU's support for British workers in struggle was unconditional.

The ITGWU played a major part in organising the wave of unrest that swept over Ireland that year. A crucial role was played by the union newspaper, the *Irish Worker*, launched on 27 May 1911 (to which we will return). Nevertheless, as Larkin's biographer, Emmet Larkin (no relation) has pointed out:

> It would be a mistake to think that all these strikes and lock-outs were confined to Dublin or those towns where Larkin and the Transport Union were in the ascendancy. The labour unrest was general throughout Ireland, and Larkin was again only a convenient focus for what was a national picture. Beginning in August 1911, the workers from one end of Ireland to the other made demands on their employers. From Jacob's biscuit factory in Dublin to the bacon factories in Limerick, from the dock labourers in Belfast to the Urban Council employees in Cork, spontaneous demands

were made and quickly conceded. Newsboys, clothing workers, golf caddies, tanners, maltsters, dairy workers and tramwaymen all clamoured for an increase in wages. The *Freeman's Journal* had to open a special column for "Irish Labour Troubles" in August to chronicle the sudden outburst of financial unrest... The general wave of strikes did not subside in Ireland until February the following year.[8]

But it was the ITGWU, under Larkin's leadership, that was to successfully transform the situation in Ireland. It was the ITGWU that established itself as a permanent outpost of working class power, challenging the interests of the employers and giving a voice to the rank and file.

The ITGWU successfully consolidated its position in the course of 1912, but did not make any further significant advances. Indeed, in May of that year Larkin was lamenting working class apathy, that the Irish workers "stand despairing, despised and inarticulate", and actually asked, "Will nothing rouse them?"[9] But the struggle continued. In the first issue of the paper that came out in 1913, he was more optimistic, editorialising that:

> 1913 seems to presage a more hopeful outlook for Labour, but as we believe God helps those who help themselves, we must determine to help ourselves, keeping in mind that success means further success. Let nothing dispirit you... Up and take your place in the ranks... Let it be a long pull and a strong pull, but all pull together. Our watchword—The World for Labour.[10]

And, indeed, 1913 was to see a renewed strike wave sweep over the country.

To begin with the union was in the ascendant. Between January and August there were over 30 strikes in Dublin. The first blow was struck by the ITGWU when over 100 dockers employed by the Dublin Steampacket Company walked out in order to impose the closed shop on their foremen. The union extended the dispute to other shipping companies, calling its members out over wages and hours, and after three months won a decisive victory. The dispute was hard fought and took a terrible toll on Larkin personally. William O'Brien remarked that he "must be made of iron to stand it so long".[11] At the end of the dispute, however, Larkin was "master of the port".[12] While this dispute was still under way, the union was involved in a bitter conflict in Sligo where the employers imported scabs from Liverpool. One striker was to be beaten to death by a scab before the dispute ended in a complete victory for the union. In Dublin County the union recruited enough farm labourers to secure an unprecedented 20 percent pay rise by the mere threat of action in August. Meanwhile in Dublin there were more disputes:

> Bottlemakers fought unavailingly for three weeks against the introduction of machines; 350 biscuit workers struck for one day for the reinstatement of a suspended worker; 500 coachbuilders were out for six weeks before they won a minimum wage; over 100 sawyers won a 50 hour week, as did 50 billposters of David Allen and Company; hairdressers struck to protest the abolition of the tipping system and their strike was honoured by the glaziers and carters of Brooks, Thomas and Company, who refused to install a pane of glass in a hairdressing establishment in sympathy with the strikers... In all, about 30 separate disputes involving over 2,200 workers, many resulting in arrests and violence, took place between January 29 and August 15.[13]

The *Irish Worker* paid particular attention to the dispute at the Savoy Confectionary Company where women workers were locked out for joining the union early in July. Every effort was made to have the company blacked with cab drivers refusing to carry scabs to and from work, carters refusing to carry goods and the company's packages being kicked off the trams. The paper printed the names and addresses of the scabs. This particular dispute was to be swallowed up by the Great Lockout.[14]

By the summer of 1913 the ITGWU had some 30,000 members and Larkin was proclaiming that Dublin was the best organised city in the world. The union seemed to be in control of events and the working class was increasingly confident and hopeful. Only the Guinness Brewery and the Dublin United Tramway Company remained as bastions of non-unionism.

Chapter 3

Larkinism

What was the nature of the labour unrest in Ireland? The Irish working class was not engaged in a revolutionary struggle for state power: Dublin in 1913 was not Petrograd in 1917, the Citizen Army was not the Red Guard and neither Larkin nor his fellow organiser James Connolly were Bolsheviks. Instead the fight in Dublin was for the right to organise, to build strong union organisation in workplaces where the employers believed they could do as they liked. It has to be insisted, however, that for the workers who fought the police in the streets, who withstood months of hardship, who defied clerical condemnation and press abuse, trade unionism had nothing to do with class collaboration or conciliation, with moderation or respectability. They were not fighting to secure knighthoods or comfortable seats in the House of Commons or even the House of Lords for their leaders. Their fight was to make the union the dominant force in the land, to break the employers' power and to make them dance to the union tune, and, ultimately, to prepare the way for the establishment of the "Industrial Commonwealth". Their struggle was what Bob Holton has called "proto-syndicalism".[15] This was a powerful component of the labour unrest in Britain too, but there it failed to overcome the entrenched resistance of the trade union leadership. The union bureaucracy was too well established in Britain and was able, although not without considerable difficulty, to contain the challenge. In Ireland, having seen off James Sexton, the movement was much more successful.

This Irish "proto-syndicalism" took the name "Larkinism". It was a multi-faceted movement made up of a combination of very diverse elements: syndicalism, industrial unionism, Labourism, revolutionary socialism, Irish republicanism, Marxism and Catholicism. Holding them all together was the principle of working class solidarity. This was the central ethic of the ITGWU, the core around which everything else revolved. Any section of workers in dispute could rely on the active support of the rest of the labour movement. Picket lines were scrupulously respected and "tainted" goods were never touched. The sympathy strike was a crucial instrument for breaking employers' resistance so that no one group of workers could ever be defeated in isolation. The intention was that eventually every worker would be enrolled in the One Big Union so that there were no divisions for employers to exploit, so that everywhere they turned they were confronted by a united working class standing shoulder to shoulder. This was the core of Larkinism and, as we have seen, by the summer of 1913 it had given the union a position of dominance in Dublin.

More generally, of course, solidarity is the only basis for a strong trade union movement where the strong and well organised can come to the assistance of those in a weaker position or confronted with particularly reactionary employers. This is why employers always want it outlawed. For Larkin and for us, solidarity has to be the watchword of a strong labour movement. This was the case in 1913; it remains the case today.

What of Larkin himself? Richard Fox, a British engineering worker and syndicalist activist, who was later to become a historian of the Irish left, described his own first encounter with Larkin when he heard him speak in London during the Lockout:

At the time I was a youth in an engineering works, feeling my life ebbing away in the workshop din and grime. Larkin expressed all my own inarticulate feeling of revolt. He did this for hundreds and thousands of young workers, and for those not so young who had been sunk in hopeless resignation. He brought colour and a sense of freedom into life...he spoke out of the heart, and the feelings to which he gave expression are still the driving force in the social struggles of today.

According to Fox, a "peculiarity of Larkin was that his speeches produced results. Many people found this hard to forgive". There were many reasonable people who pointed out that social conditions in Dublin were appalling, indeed intolerable, but "they could do nothing to alter conditions before Larkin started his movement. The employers were impervious to reason... So Larkin spoke in the only language they could understand". This was the language of militancy and class struggle. As far as "the mass of working people" were concerned, Larkin was "their standard bearer in the struggle". He was "a scathing, exultant tornado of a man".[16]

What of Larkin's weaknesses? When we examine Larkin's politics during this period it is clear that he held to two different, indeed contradictory, strategies for achieving socialism that existed side by side. On the one hand, he was the advocate of trade union struggle and of the One Big Union, of workers building up their strength on the job until industry was effectively in their hands whereupon they could finally take over production, by means of a general strike if necessary. This was a syndicalist strategy. On the other hand, he also advocated the establishment of an Irish Labour Party, a reformist party, which would be controlled by the trade union movement, which would contest elections and which would eventually take power by constitutional means. The employing class was the enemy that had to be defeated in struggle, while the state was seen as a neutral agency that could be captured through the ballot box.

Today the weaknesses of this sort of politics are clear. Larkin's belief that that the union was the weapon that could defeat the capitalist class did not recognise the unevenness of working class consciousness. While the union must organise *all* workers, the most politically advanced workers need to be organised as the political leadership of the class, in a revolutionary party. And he did not recognise that the capitalist state had to be smashed rather than captured. Whatever power the workers had succeeded in building up in the workplace would be attacked by the capitalist state in order to protect the capitalist system. The establishment of socialism required not an electoral victory or even a general strike but an armed insurrection. This was a lesson Marx had drawn in the 1870s, and which revolutionary socialists such as Lenin were developing in the early 20th century. Larkinism remained a movement that could extract concessions from the employers, that could put them on the defensive, but it never provided an adequate strategy for socialist transformation. While strikes could bring individual or even groups of employers to heel, any attempt at overthrowing capitalism itself would inevitably confront the capitalist state, and this Larkin, along with the rest of the left in both Britain and Ireland, was not prepared for at this time. The state was a separate matter and would be captured through the ballot box.

Even Jim Connolly, one of the foremost Marxist thinkers of the time, the ITGWU's Belfast organiser when the Lockout began, who was to become Larkin's chief lieutenant as the struggle continued, advocated essentially similar politics. Connolly had played a leading role in attempts at building socialist organisations in Britain, Ireland and the US. In the 1890s and early 1900s his politics were essentially those of the American Daniel De Leon and his Socialist Labor Party. De Leon emphasised the importance of building industrial unions (he helped found the Industrial Workers of the World (IWW) in 1905 and for a while Connolly had been an IWW organiser in the US) although he was insistent that they had to be kept under party control. Connolly eventually broke with De Leon's sectarian conception of a revolutionary party, but he never developed an alternative of his own. Instead, as far as Connolly was concerned, the syndicalist trade union was the instrument for the overthrow of capitalism. But alongside this he supported the establishment of an Irish Labour Party. Indeed, he proposed the resolution establishing it at the Irish Trades Union Congress in 1912. Connolly also saw the need for a separate Socialist Party of Ireland, a propagandist organisation, arguing socialist politics and developing Marxist ideas.

Both Larkin and Connolly saw the ITGWU as a weapon in the class struggle, as a club with which to beat the employers into submission and thereby prepare the way for socialism which would be finally achieved by means of an electoral victory. It was only after the Russian Revolution of 1917 that their particular combination of syndicalism and electoralism was to be superseded. The Bolsheviks were to transform revolutionary politics throughout the world.

Chapter 4

The *Irish Worker*

The character of Larkinism is best captured in the pages of the ITGWU's weekly newspaper, the *Irish Worker*. According to Larkin's biographer:

> Nothing like it has ever been seen since it was suppressed by the British government in the early months of the First World War. This novel production was and remains unique in the history of working class journalism. It was less a newspaper than the spirit of four glorious years. To read the *Irish Worker* of these years is to feel the quickening pulse of Dublin. Week after week...Larkin attacked, with a monumental perseverance, the sweating, exploiting employers and the corrupt, cynical politicians who in his eyes were responsible for the reprehensible social conditions in Dublin. He gave no quarter and expected none as he vilified any and all, high or low, who had the misfortune to come under the notice of his pen.[17]

Robert Lowery, in his study of Sean O'Casey's involvement with the ITGWU, has emphasised Larkin's personal contribution to the paper's success:

> As a writer, he authored nearly 400 articles over a 41-month period. Every week he wrote one or more editorials which were fresh and lively and, as often as not, explosive. Readers could always expect something which would move them one way or the other. One week it might be a stirring tribute to Robert Emmet, Wolfe Tone or St Patrick. The next week might feature a blistering attack on a sweatshop employer

or a scathing denunciation of a local politician who had been caught padding his payroll with his relatives. The number of articles written by Larkin is staggering when one realises that he was also in charge of the Irish Transport and General Workers Union, president of the Irish Women Workers Union, a frequent candidate for political office and often the main speaker at workers' rallies in all parts of Ireland... As an editor, Larkin must be judged a success.[18]

The first issue appeared on 27 May 1911 and sold some 5,000 copies. The following week's issue sold 8,000 and the next around 15,000, before finally settling at some 20,000 copies a week. Readers were urged to pass the paper on to their friends and workmates. As Charles Desmond Greaves observed, the *Irish Worker* "was read or discussed by the entire working class of the city. This was something unprecedented in any city in the world".[19] Richard Fox wrote of the paper that:

> Everyone knew which side it was on. It had warm-hearted generous praise for friends but for scabs, employers who paid low wages and denied the right of trade union organisation, enemies of every description, it had nothing but a stream of abuse. This paper kept up the fighting spirit. Larkin, though always weak as a theorist—he had not the slightest interest in theory—was a master of smashing technique when it came to labour struggle. This was a time when struggle was very necessary and Larkin was the man in the gap.[20]

Chapter 5

Preaching discontent

From its very first issue the *Irish Worker* preached discontent and rebellion, urging its readers to join together in the fight for better wages and living conditions, for a free Ireland and for a new social order. The paper was, in the best traditions of the left press, an educator and an organiser, a paper that raised the spirits and rallied its readers in the struggle for a better world. In his 1911 editorial, "A Call to Arms", Larkin wrote that the recent skirmishes between "Labour and Capitalism in Ireland" had given the workers:

> a foretaste of how your bowelless masters regard you. Their kept press spewed foul lies, innuendoes, and gave space to the knaves of our own class for the purpose of garrotting our glorious movement. At present you spend your lives in sordid labour and have your abode in filthy slums; your children hunger, and your masters say your slavery must endure for ever. If you would come out of bondage yourself must forge the weapons and fight the grim battle... The *Irish Worker* will be a lamp to light your feet in the dark hours of the impending struggle, a well of truth reflecting the purity of your motives, and a weekly banquet from which you will rise strengthened in purpose to emulate the deeds of your forefathers, who died in dungeon and on scaffold in the hopes for a glorious resurrection for our beloved country.

Over the three and a half years of its existence the paper carried regular detailed exposures of the terrible social conditions that existed in Dublin where the poverty and slum conditions were the worst in Western Europe. On 11 November 1911 the front page was devoted to R J P Mortished's "Facts About Dublin", a statistical account of poverty in the city, written by a socialist civil servant. From 4 May until 15 June 1912 it serialised Jim Connolly's "Labour and the Reconquest of Ireland" on the front page. And over five weeks spanning August and September that same year it carried Andrew Patrick Wilson's (he wrote under the pseudonym "Euchan") series on "Labour and Frugality". Wilson was a Scottish socialist and actor, working at the Abbey theatre in Dublin, a regular contributor to the paper and a strong supporter of the ITGWU.[21] In the "Labour and Frugality" articles Wilson demonstrated that, no matter how careful they were, the wages of unskilled workers were just not enough to live on. In the last of the series that appeared in the paper on 14 September, Wilson called for the introduction of a "living wage" and explained how to get it (a still very relevant question!):

> It can be obtained by the workers themselves without thanks to anyone. Let the workers stand firmly together, shoulder to shoulder, just as the masters do. Let the demand come from all—one union for all workers, and the capitalist class could not resist... The workers are not making the class war, for the class war has been forced upon them. Let the workers learn from the masters how to engage in the fight. Federation! Consolidation! Organisation! These are the watchwords for the workers—the three-leafed Shamrock of Labour growing from one stalk—the one great union for all workers.

The only way to ensure a living wage under capitalism was through the strength and power of the trade union movement.

These broad, general critiques of class society were accompanied by exposés of individual cases of injustice and exploitation that dramatised the nature of class relations in the city. Larkin, as the socialist journalist W P Ryan observed, always "called ugly things by their names".[22] A couple of examples will give a flavour of this aspect of Larkin's writing. In January 1912 the paper reported the callous and inhumane treatment of John Carroll at the hands of Jameson's Distillery, where he had worked for 45 years. Now aged 102, Carroll still worked as a sandwichboard man, but every Christmas he received a Christmas box from his former employer. Every Christmas the *Irish Worker* had a party for Dublin's 200 impoverished sandwichboard men and at the end of the 1911 celebration it had fallen to John Carroll to propose the vote of thanks. When he subsequently turned up at Jameson's for his Christmas box, he was told that the firm knew about his association with the *Irish Worker* and he was turned away empty handed and told "he could go and make speeches for a living". The paper launched a collection for him.

Let us look at one other example from the *Irish Worker* of 24 May 1913. Here Larkin told his readers of how a poverty-stricken mother had brought her two girls, aged 14 and 16, to see him. They worked for a clothing firm, Somersets, and had received 10p for 12 days' work. The girls had shown him "their docket issued by these soulless blood-suckers". Starting out from this particular heart-breaking injustice, Larkin went on to warn Dublin's employers that:

> the time is rapidly arriving when you will be called to a halt! The *Worker* is doing its share in educating the working class to their own want of knowledge, want of class loyalty, want of earnestness, want of spirit, and their rights which they have forgotten to demand. A new nation is in birth, a newer type of man and woman is being formed among the working class; a new era opens out to us, and the *Worker* is one of the instruments to that end—the end being a mutual Commonwealth built on service, a broadening out of the

perspective of life, a fuller and more complete life, the oblit-
erating of class rule and distinction of caste—a day when
work, useful and beautiful, will be the test; when the idler,
the wastrel, the fop, the creature of an hour shall cease to be,
and the builder, the beautifier shall take their rightful place
in the land...there will be no child slaves in those good days
to be working 12 days for ten pence.

Clearly, the ITGWU was not just about higher wages,
but about the transformation and overthrow of capitalist
society. A Mutual Commonwealth was the objective.

The paper turned its fire on individual employers, with
the Quaker biscuit manufacturer, George Jacob, being a particular favourite. The abuse poured on his head was, however,
nothing compared to that dished out to Catholic Ireland's
foremost capitalist, William Martin Murphy. He had exten-
sive business interests in Ireland, Britain, South America and
West Africa. He controlled the Dublin United Tramway
Company owned the city's largest hotel, the Imperial,
along with Clery's department store. He also owned the
Independent newspaper group, which was used to protect
his other business interests and to oppose the advance of
the labour movement and, in particular, the ITGWU. He
was, as Larkin put it, "a toady, a renegade, an untruthful
and dishonest politician, a false friend, a sweating employer,
a weak-kneed tyrant...a whited sepulchre".[23] According to
Andrew Patrick Wilson, even his own mother turned away
from him "with a shudder of revulsion".[24] And, as Larkin
complained, "this modern capitalistic vampire" used his
newspaper empire to attack the labour movement. Murphy
employed "a group of journalistic renegades, whose bodies
and souls he controls. They write the most foul, vicious and
lying tirades against the working class at so much a column".
The workers, he warned, would not soon forget the "paid
blacklegs of the press".[25]

This written abuse was reinforced by the paper's cartoons, in particular those drawn by James Kavanagh, whose visual portrayal of Murphy was to do the man immense damage. In the Christmas 1913 issue, during the Great Lockout, Kavanagh portrayed Murphy as a "Bad Santa", delivering gifts of starvation and disease to the children of the working class. This was powerful stuff.[26]

Chapter 6

For national freedom

One aspect of the *Irish Worker*'s politics that does not get enough emphasis is its support for the establishment of an Irish Republic, but a republic where the workers would rule. The paper carried as its masthead the declaration of one of the Irish republican leaders of the 1840s, James Fintan Lalor, the editor of the *Irish Felon* newspaper: "The principle I state and mean to stand upon is that the entire ownership of Ireland, moral and material, up to the sun and down to the centre is vested of right in the people of Ireland." Over a nine-week period in the summer of 1911, during the visit to Ireland of the British king, George V, Larkin reprinted articles from the *Felon*, reminding its readers of the Great Famine and of the 1848 Rebellion. When the king visited Dublin in July 1911, the paper celebrated the more than a thousand people who rallied at Wolfe Tone's graveside in Bodenstown "in preference to staying in the city to watch the procession". These people made it clear that they cared more for republican principles "than they did for all the tawdry pomp and bloody vengeance of the Pirate Empire". The paper insisted that:

> The welfare of the people of Ireland is more important to us than the smiles of a king or a queen. While there is a hungry man, woman or child in Ireland, while there is even one of our people ill-clad or ill-treated, we will join no display of hypocritical loyalty. While there is one barefooted child in this country we cannot afford to buy flags or fireworks, nor present loyal addresses.[27]

As for Home Rule, the limited scheme of devolution that the Home Rule party championed at this time, any idea that this was the final settlement of Ireland's national claims was subjected to ferocious ridicule by the paper. It was a betrayal of the past generation who had fought and died for Irish freedom. And when it became clear that partition, the separation of the North from the rest of the country, was the price of Home Rule, the *Irish Worker* responded with disbelieving outrage. As far as Larkin was concerned, partition was all about keeping the working class divided and setting them against one another by means of "the same methods that were used one hundred years ago to divide the common people".[28] The paper condemned this attempt to create "two distinct Irelands", warning that it would condemn the Irish people "for generations to come" to fight among themselves "rather than in a combined effort to lift the toilers of all creeds to a position of affluence in the land of their birth". One interesting point is that the *Irish Worker* put much of the blame for all this on Catholic sectarianism, in particular on the Ancient Order of Hibernians.[29] If it were not for the Hibernians and the fear of a Catholic supremacy that their activities gave rise to, the *Worker* argued, "the Orange Society would have long since ceased to exist". British politicians "must feel deeply indebted to the Hibernian president for placing such an effective check upon the fusion of Orange and Green that was rapidly taking place amongst the workers of Ulster". Instead the paper urged "a united Ireland, the Ireland of Tone, Emmet and McCracken"—all three Protestant republicans as its readers would have known.[30] While this blaming of Protestant sectarianism on the Hibernians certainly demonstrates the ITGWU's determined stand against Catholic sectarianism, it was completely inadequate as an explanation for developments in the North.

The *Irish Worker* was, at this time, the most powerful voice of republicanism in Ireland, dwarfing in circulation other republican publications. It championed a socialist working class republicanism and anti-imperialism, urging that only with the establishment of an Irish Republic would the workers be able to bring about a socialist reordering of Irish society. Moreover, the paper insisted, it had always been the working class who were in the forefront of the struggle for freedom. On one occasion Larkin celebrated the memory of the "Manchester Martyrs", Allen, Larkin and O'Brien, hanged after a policeman was killed during the rescue of a Fenian leader in Manchester in September 1867. They were "those three humble working men, who gave their all for the Irish nation". And to the question of whether their actions were justified or not: "We say emphatically, yes." He promised that "we will never disgrace nor forget you".[31]

In early January 1913 the *Irish Worker* published a front page article, "New Year's Thoughts for Ireland", considering the national question's relationship to the class struggle. "We do not deny", the paper argued, "that in most cases the cause of Labour is the same the whole world over", but in Ireland there was also "a clear national issue...one that deserves a clear and distinct answer". While Dublin, for example, was certainly "rotten...the refuge of a capitalistic snobocracy; full of prigs and shoneens; and polite poltroons", nevertheless "we want the workingmen to Irishize it". The fact was that the working class was "ever in the forefront of the fight for freedom" and always "bore the brunt of the battle", that "the national forces of Ireland were ever composed mainly of workingmen", and that "if there is a future in Ireland it is the workingmen who will achieve it". But, the paper promised, while "our class...cannot be false to our country, neither can we be false to our class outside the nation".[32]

One last point worth making here is that there has been a tendency to associate working class nationalism in this period with Jim Connolly, as if he invented it. In fact, there was a long tradition of working class commitment to the national cause dating back to the 1790s (when it had widespread support among Protestant workers in the North) and carrying on through 1848 and the 1860s.[33] What Connolly did was to root this nationalism in Marxist theory in his great book, *Labour in Irish History*.

Chapter 7

The Lockout begins

As 1913 progressed, the ITGWU's strength was such that the Dublin Employers Federation agreed to the establishment of a Board of Conciliation. This was a reluctant recognition of the success of the union's militancy. The employers were desperate to avoid strikes that they were fated to lose through the exercise of working class solidarity. Whereas they had once routinely broken strikes and victimised "ringleaders", now they sought terms. The ITGWU pressed for full recognition of the unions and for the closed shop if 80 percent of a workforce joined the union. As Larkin put it, while "the ultimate solution is the ownership and control of the means of life by the whole people," this would do for the moment.[34]

All that remained for Dublin to be a union city was the organisation of the Dublin United Tramway Company and the defeat of William Martin Murphy. Pay was low, hours were long and conditions were bad on the trams. Drivers and conductors only had one day off in 12, and sometimes they lost that, and the working day was at least 12 hours long and often longer with no overtime pay. There was a regime of petty regulations enforced by informers (these creatures received 2/6d a week extra in their pay packets), draconian fines and punishments. When starting work for the company, men had to work for six weeks without pay and without any days off for a year to see if they were suitable. And there was a pool of casual employees who were required to turn up each morning to see if any of the regular men were absent whereupon they would be taken on and paid. When a driver or conductor left or was sacked his replacement came from among this casual pool. A worker who offended the management in some way might well find himself returned to the pool. Unrest was widespread among the tramway men but it was kept suppressed by fear.[35]

The ITGWU began to build support among the tramway men and Larkin hoped to have recruited a majority of them before confronting the management. In the event of a strike being necessary, the union had every reason to believe that solidarity action, blacking and mass picketing would shut the trams down and bring Murphy to heel. Indeed so alarmed was Murphy that he actually held a meeting with the workers where their pay was increased by a shilling a week and new men were given one day off in 12 from the time they started. He warned that the company would spend £100,000 to defeat Larkin, but would recognise a "legitimate" union. The Ancient Order of Hibernians was brought in to set up a "yellow" or scab union. The ITGWU continued to recruit and so Murphy decided on confrontation.

Murphy recognised that two factors were essential if he was to defeat the ITGWU. First, he needed the wholehearted support of the authorities in the form of sufficient police and, if necessary, troops, to keep scab trams running. And on 22 August the Dublin press reported that the Tramway Company had been "assured of the most ample protection of their men by the forces of the Crown".[36] Such open backing from the authorities would make possible the second requirement which was the mobilisation of Dublin's employers against the union. Once the employers realised that the government was wholeheartedly behind an attack on the ITGWU, they suddenly became brave enough to take the union on. Working class solidarity that had allowed the union to take a grip on the city was to be met with a general lockout that would smash the ITGWU once and for all. Despite having only recently agreed to the establishment of a Board of Conciliation, the Dublin Employers Federation was to follow Murphy's lead and attempt to crush the trade union movement in the city. And the assault was given the blessing of the Liberal government in London and its representative in Dublin, Augustine Birrell MP.

Murphy struck first before the union had finished its preparations. On 19 August he fired all the union members working in the despatch department of his *Irish Independent* newspaper and two days later he fired some 200 men and boys working in the parcels department of the Tramway Company for refusing to handle his newspapers. Before he could conduct a similar purge of his drivers and conductors, Larkin struck back. The union put in a demand for a significant pay rise, one day off in eight and time and a half for Sunday working. It was ignored and the men walked off the job on 26 August, the second day of the Dublin Horse Show, when the city was full of visitors. To achieve the maximum impact they stopped work at 10am, abandoning their trams and passengers in the street. Some 700 men walked out—not as many as had been hoped, but they were still confident of victory. The union was strong enough to defeat Murphy. Mass picketing and solidarity action would stop the trams and this would lead to more men joining the winning side.

The Dublin Castle authorities moved quickly to provide a public demonstration of their support for Murphy. On 28 August, Larkin and other union leaders were arrested for seditious libel, seditious conspiracy and unlawful assembly. A union protest was called for Sunday 28 August in O'Connell Street, but was promptly banned. Larkin made clear his intention of defying the ban by publicly burning the police proclamation and then went into hiding to avoid re-arrest.

Crucial to Murphy's success in persuading other employers to join in the attack on the ITGWU was the role of the police. According to the *Irish Times* they were "straining at the leash".[37] The police were set loose to baton the union and its supporters off the streets. In Jim Phelan's words, the police launched "an attack upon Dublin exactly comparable to a military assault by an enemy". He remembered how "at almost any hour of the day or night, one might run into a bitter and bloody fight between a body of Constabulary and a group of citizens". You could "expect to be bludgeoned anywhere, at any time".[38] Over the weekend of 30 and 31 August the police ran riot, batoning the working class off the streets, beating three men—John Byrne, James Nolan, and James Carey—to death and seriously injuring hundreds more.[39] They stormed into the tenements, beating men, women and children, wrecking furniture and destroying possessions. On the Sunday morning, when Larkin staged a token defiance of the ban on the O'Connell Street protest (he appeared on the balcony of Murphy's Imperial Hotel), as soon as the crowd of bystanders and sympathisers began cheering him, the police attacked everyone in the vicinity—workers and the more respectable members of Dublin society. And whereas previously the worst of their brutality had taken place at night, now they showed what they were made of in broad daylight on a public thoroughfare. A Liberal MP visiting the city, Handel Booth, described the police as "the most brutal constabulary ever let loose on a peaceful assembly". The police behaved like "men possessed" and he saw people desperately trying to escape "knocked senseless...kicking the victims when prostrate was a settled part of the police programme".[40] As the fighting spread throughout the city, the police once again raided the tenements, determined to teach the working class a lesson they would not forget. In their attack on Corporation Buildings the police invaded the home of John McDonagh, who was paralysed and confined to his bed. They beat him as he lay there and clubbed his wife when she intervened. He died later in hospital.[41]

This was the start of a protracted battle for the streets that was to last for months. Jim Phelan remembered how the police came to curse "the alleys where people used such unsporting engines as eye-pepper, hat-pins or broken glass in socks".[42] So effective were attacks on scab trams that the service had to be discontinued at dusk. When wrecked trams were sent to the Inchicore coach works, a Larkinite stronghold, for repair, the coach builders blacked them and were promptly locked out. And as for those workers who appeared in court charged with public order offences, "Sentences of from one to three months were passed on prisoners who appeared battered, bandaged and black-eyed".[43]

Jim Connolly was already in prison on 31 August "learning", as he put it, "to walk around in a ring with about 40 other unfortunates kept six paces apart". As union members were brought in to serve their time, he asked them what they were in for: "For throwing stones at the police." When he made clear his support for such activities and his hope that their aim had been good, he was told that in fact they had not had the chance to attack the police because had been "pulled" outside their homes and imprisoned on perjured evidence.[44] Acquittal was virtually unheard of, although a certain Christopher Nolan had to have charges of throwing stones at the police dismissed, despite two police officers clearly identifying him, because he was already in prison when he was supposed to have committed the offence![45] The workers remained defiant, however. Larkin told the story of one 17 year old union member who appeared in court and was sentenced to one month's hard labour. As she was led from the dock, she called out, "Three cheers for Jim Larkin", and was promptly called back up and given another month. As she was again taken down she once more called out, "Three cheers for Jim Larkin", but this time the magistrate let her defiance pass.[46] By the time the dispute was over, more than 400 men and women, including most of the union leadership, were to serve time for offences related to the Lockout, and one union officer, James Byrne, chairman of Kingstown Trades Council, was to die from the after-effects of hunger strike. Byrne has been almost forgotten, but Connolly memorialised him at the time as a man "murdered...for the sacred cause of liberty" by the "police vultures and the master vultures".[47]

The Great Lockout began on 1 September when the first workers at Jacob's biscuits were fired for wearing the union's Red Hand badge to work. That night there were clashes "outside the biscuit factory... The shop windows were smashed and additional police had to be called up".[48] By the end of the week over 3,000 Jacob's workers, overwhelmingly women, had been locked out. On 2 September the coal merchants locked out their workers for refusing to repudiate their membership of the ITGWU. Firm after firm followed suit until by the end of the month some 25,000 workers had been locked out by over 400 employers. The attack on the ITGWU had escalated into an attack on the whole Dublin labour movement, with the members of another 28 unions being locked out. In the building trade the Labourers' Union was told to provide undertakings not to support the ITGWU and refused. As Connolly reported, "all over Dublin their 2,500 members marched out 'to help the ITGWU boys'."[49]

Throughout the city over the following weeks employers confronted their workers with the Dublin Employers Federation's notorious document: "I hereby undertake to carry out all instructions given by or on behalf of my employers, and further I agree to immediately resign membership of the ITGWU (if a member) and I further undertake that I will not join or in any way support this union".[50] The intention was clear: the ITGWU was to be destroyed and the Dublin labour movement crippled. On 1 September Murphy addressed the Dublin Chamber of Commerce. He told an audience of cheering business men to be of good heart because in 99 cases out of 100 strikes were defeated. The fact was that in any strike the employer "all the time managed to get his three meals a day, but the unfortunate workman and his family had no resources whatever except submission". He did confess, however, that the "difficulty of teaching that lesson to the workman was extraordinary".[51]

The city was filled with police and troops. Attempts at mass picketing were broken up by violent police attacks and any attempt at peaceful picketing saw pickets assaulted and, if they complained, arrested and imprisoned. Instead "picketing became a part of hit-and-run guerrilla tactics". Larkin urged that union members should make every effort to ensure that the police really earned their pay during the dispute.[52] Men went armed to meetings and demonstrations in order to protect themselves from police attack. In Inchicore, where Larkin was due to speak, the rumour spread that the police intended to break the meeting up. The men working in the local foundry "collected iron bolts and bars from the furnace scrap. Some came with lumps of heavy gas pipe". The meeting passed off without trouble, however, and as the crowd dispersed they abandoned their weaponry in the street. The police were able to fill a hand-cart with the scrap.[53]

The ITGWU's militant temper at this time is perhaps best captured by Andrew Patrick Wilson's song, "Who Fears To Wear The Blood Red Badge?", that appeared in the *Irish Worker* on 11 October 1913:

> Who fears to wear the blood red badge
> Upon his manly breast?
> What scab obeys the vile command
> Of Murphy and the rest?
> He's all a knave and half a slave
> Who slights his Union thus,
> But true men, like you men,
> Will show the badge with us.

They dared to fling a manly brick,
That wrecked a blackleg tram,
They dared give Harvey Duff* a kick,
They didn't care a damn,
They lie in gaol and can't get bail
Who fought their corner thus,
But you men, with sticks men,
Must make the Peelers cuss.

We rise in sad and weary days
To fight the workers' cause,
We found in Jim, a heart ablaze
To break down unjust laws,
But 'tis a sin to follow him,
Says Murphy and his crew,
But you men, like true men,
Will stick to him like glue.

Good luck be with him. He is here
To win for us this fight,
To suffer for us without fear,
To champion the right.
So stick to Jim, let nothing dim
Our ardour in the fray,
And true Jim, our own Jim,
Will win our fight today.

(*Harvey Duff was a fictional police informer in Dion Boucicault's popular drama, *The Shaughraun*.)

The "Blood Red Badge" was the ITGWU's Red Hand badge that was issued to members. As for Murphy, he was so grateful to the police for their assistance that he gave them the right when off-duty to travel free on the trams, a right they retained until 1938.

Chapter 8

Solidarity and food ships

On 2 September William Partridge, representing the Dublin Trades Council, crossed over to Manchester to address the British Trades Union Congress about the crisis. He told the delegates that the Dublin workers were "not merely struggling for the cause of trade unionism, but are actually defending their lives and the lives of those dear to them". He was a skilled engineer, a member of the Amalgamated Society of Engineers (ASE), but he told the delegates the skilled trades recognised that Murphy was not just attacking the ITGWU, but had "declared war on the trade unions" and that the defeat of the ITGWU "would mean the destruction of trade unionism throughout the length and breadth of Ireland".[54] According to Harry Gosling, one of the delegates and a full-time official, "Ireland was in all our minds."

After hearing Partridge speak, the congress decided that same day to send a delegation (including Gosling) to Dublin. They found the city "under a semi-military regime with the whole population terrorised". Together with the ITGWU and the Dublin Trades Council, the delegation decided to help assert the labour movement's right to free speech and to demonstrate by holding a demonstration down O'Connell Street. On Sunday 7 September the right to demonstrate was reasserted, despite the authorities warning the TUC delegation that "we were taking our lives into our own hands". An "immense crowd" started out from Liberty Hall, it blocked "the whole of Abbey Street as far as the eye could see" and by the time they reached O'Connell Street "it was packed with men". To tremendous cheers resolutions were passed asserting the right to demonstrate, the right to picket and the right to union recognition. The police were noticeable by their absence.[55]

While the TUC delegation offered welcome assistance, the intention of the official leadership of the British trade union movement was to settle the dispute as quickly as possible—over the heads of the ITGWU membership if necessary. They regarded Larkin as unnecessarily provocative and were prepared to make substantial concessions to the employers to end the dispute. Their efforts were unsuccessful because Murphy and co were not interested in any sort of compromise; they wanted the complete destruction of the ITGWU. The struggle went on.

From the very beginning of the Lockout there were workers in Britain eager to black traffic from Dublin. The ITGWU had scrupulously supported British workers in struggle and many British workers—dockers, transport workers and railwaymen—were keen to reciprocate. The murderous brutality of the police assault on the Dublin workers had been widely reported in the British press, particularly in the *Daily Herald*. The *Herald* was, at this time, very much the paper of the rank and file trade union militant, was very critical of the moderation of trade union officialdom and urged solidarity action, unofficial if necessary. There was a network of Herald Leagues throughout the country, that supported strikes and protests, and this was to provide the basis for a concerted effort to mount solidarity action in support of the Dublin workers. According to Richard Fox, who was an enthusiastic member of the league, its "all-comprehensive motto was 'Unite and Fight'". It was, he recalled, not thought necessary to have a more definite programme, because there were "so many fights going on just then".[56] On 16 September railwaymen in Liverpool, the scene of a militant general strike only two years earlier,[57] refused to handle Dublin traffic and the dispute quickly spread down the tracks as far as Birmingham, Sheffield, Derby and beyond. Rather than touch tainted goods, railwaymen either walked out or were locked out. All this was completely unofficial, cheered on by the *Daily Herald*. It was the work of rank and file militants who were fighting for a more combative stance in their own unions. For a time it looked as if a national railwaymen's stoppage in support of the Dublin workers was on the cards, but the full-time officials managed to secure a return to work.

What of the British Marxist left during the Lockout? The largest Marxist organisation in Britain at this time was the British Socialist Party (BSP), which claimed a membership of 40,000 in 370 branches in 1912. The BSP had begun life as the Social Democratic Federation, established in 1884. In its early years it had been distinctly unsympathetic to trade union struggle, which was seen as a diversion from the propagandist effort at winning people over to socialism and achieving electoral victory. According to the party's historian, this attitude had prevented it "from seizing the opportunities offered by the upsurge of New Unionism" in the late 1880s and early 1890s. This stance did undergo some modification over the years, but party leader Henry Hyndman's boast in February 1912 that he had "never advocated a strike" hardly inspired confidence. There were revolutionaries in the BSP, men and women, often influenced by syndicalist ideas, who wanted to fight the employers, but the leadership remained lukewarm towards industrial struggle, ferociously opposed to syndicalist ideas and wedded to the official movement.[58]

When the Dublin Lockout began, however, the BSP gave its full support to the ITGWU and urged its members to organise solidarity meetings throughout Britain. On Sunday 7 September the London Trades Council and the BSP, which had a strong influence on that body, jointly sponsored a protest meeting in Trafalgar Square in support of the Dublin workers. The meeting was backed by the whole

London labour movement, including the Labour Party. According to the BSP's newspaper, *Justice*, it was "some years since so large a crowd assembled in Trafalgar Square". There was "fierce indignation at the atrocities committed by the police in the Irish capital". The report went on:

> About a quarter of an hour after the meeting had started, the arrival of the East End contingent made a profound impression. At the sound of the band playing the "Dead March" every head was bared, and when the strains of the "Marseillaise" followed the whole crowd seemed to unite in a great defiant cheer.

Among the speakers that day was the British dockers' leader, Ben Tillett, who made a typically militant and uncompromising speech. The hero of the hour, however, was William Partridge, speaking for the Dublin Trades Council: "He spoke with grim and biting humour of the previous week's outrages, and of the attempt to kill Irish trade unionism and to suppress free speech." That same Sunday the BSP held public protest meetings in support of the Dublin workers across much of the country. *Justice* reported meetings in Newcastle, Plymouth, Salford, Birmingham, Coventry, Bristol, Lincoln, Whitehaven, Leicester, Hull, Oxford, Burnley, Gloucester, Newport, Eastbourne, Bradford, Woolwich, Portsmouth, Greenock and Colne.[59]

The limitations of the party's approach soon showed themselves, however. On 4 October 1913, the party newspaper, *Justice*, complained that while there was "class bitterness" in Dublin, there was little "socialist propaganda". Socialist politics was not really needed while the struggle was actually under way, the paper argued, but once it was settled they could come to the fore. Indeed, "the more active part Socialists take...the more readily they will be listened to afterwards when they tell the workers what to do and what to avoid". On 11 October an editorial in *Justice*, "The Labour

Unrest and the Duty of Socialists", insisted that whatever their limitations, unionised workers were "superior in every way to those who are unorganised". Nevertheless, the fact was there was not much benefit for the working class from this "outburst of strike fever". All it was likely to result in was "the depleted state of the funds of the many unions engaged in those strikes rather than in any material improvement in the conditions of the workers themselves". Despite this, socialists had to support the workers because, "however much we may wish they would use different methods, they are in the right and the employers are in the wrong". This was hardly a call to arms. The real problem, however, was that as a growing rank and file revolt against the trade union bureaucracy developed, the BSP absolutely unequivocally took the side of the trade union bureaucracy, condemning unofficial action, the activities of the "rank and vile", and even warning of agents provocateurs, imported from America, trying to undermine the movement. The paper turned its fire on the syndicalists, both in its own ranks and outside, condemning the influence of the *Daily Herald* that was apparently leading Jim Larkin astray. Indeed, *Justice* proclaimed that there had never been a dispute "where the leaders and the rank and file of the unions have been so completely at one as in this Dublin lock-out".[60] In the end the BSP failed the test in 1913. It was the *Daily Herald* that rallied trade union militants and activists behind the Dublin workers in defiance of the trade union leadership.

While the leaders of the British trade union movement resolutely set their faces against any industrial action in support of the Dublin workers (they wanted good relations with the employers, not confrontation), they were prepared to provide them with considerable financial support. Clearly this was one way to head off rank and file demands for industrial action and would also strengthen the TUC's hand in its dealings with the ITGWU, in its attempts to force the Irish union to retreat, but nevertheless the effort put in to raising funds for the Dublin workers was pretty tremendous. By the time the Lockout was over, the British labour movement had donated some £150,000 (over £11 million in today's money) to the Dublin workers. Most of this was donated by trade unions (the Miners Federation gave £14,000, the ASE gave £4,000 and The National Union of Teachers gave £1,000, and so on), but considerable sums were also raised by street collections, at rallies and meetings and from individuals. We shall return to this.

To dramatise the British movement's solidarity, the TUC organised the despatch of food ships, bringing relief to the Dublin workers in very public displays of support. The first British food ship, the *Hare*, arrived in Dublin on 27 September. According to Harry Gosling, who was on board, the reception they received in Dublin left them "dumb, with tears in our eyes. It was the most wonderful sight I have ever seen". The cargo of 60,000 food packages had been prepared by the Cooperative Wholesale Society. By midnight all the packages had been distributed.[61] Other ships followed, with the Christmas ship, the *Fraternity*, arriving in Dublin on 17 December, carrying presents and sweets for the locked out workers' children, as well as the regular food supplies. The last food ship was despatched on 3 February 1914. By the time the Lockout came to an end, the food ships had carried 1,797,699 loaves of bread, 689,166 10lb bags of potatoes, 472,966 packets of margarine, 480,306 packets of tea, 461,530 packets of sugar, 72,830 jars of jam, 12,500 packets of cheese, 2,400 cans of condensed milk, 884 tons of coal and more at a total cost of £62,889.[62] Murphy's newspapers somewhat predictably described the food ships as a British plot to bankrupt Dublin's shopkeepers!

The *Daily Herald* and the Herald Leagues were particularly active in collecting money. Meetings in support of the Dublin workers were held all over Britain. Collections were taken and often auctions were held when donated items would be sold off to raise money. On one occasion at a meeting in Finsbury Park in London the summonses that four men had received for holding a street collection for the Dublin workers were auctioned off. On another occasion a captured police truncheon was auctioned.[63] Harry McShane, the veteran Glasgow socialist, remembered 1913 as the only time actual street collections were organised for workers in dispute. He got involved after he ran "into old Willie McGill taking a strike collection using a barrel-organ...I offered to help". They went out "every Saturday night, collecting money in the streets and round all the theatre queues...we collected at least a couple of pounds".[64]

Without any doubt, this financial assistance was crucial in allowing the ITGWU to continue the fight over the long months of the Lockout. Indeed, so low was the pay and so irregular the work of many of the union's members that they and their families were better fed during the Lockout than when they were working. Jim Connolly freely acknowledged that "the huge amount of money...raised" in Britain allowed "the men and women of Dublin to keep the fight going". As far as he was concerned, at this moment, "the working class of Great Britain reached its highest point of moral grandeur".[65] At the end of October, however, the Dublin employers began to import hundreds of scabs from Britain. On 6 November the first shipload of scabs arrived to be soon followed by others. The employers were determined to break the deadlock. More police and troops were drafted into the city to protect the strikebreakers who were also liberally supplied with licensed firearms. Financial support was no longer enough. It was in response to this deteriorating situation that Larkin was to launch his "Fiery Crusade" in Britain, appealing for the blacking of Dublin traffic.

Chapter 9

The church intervenes

Before we consider these developments, however, it is worth looking at the children's holiday scheme that the ITGWU organised and at the way the Catholic church used it to try and wreck the workers' cause. The Catholic church in Ireland was not pro-British in its sympathies at this time but was a strong supporter of the Home Rule party; indeed, there were many priests, including William Walsh, the Archbishop of Dublin, who did not think that the Home Rule party was nationalist enough. It was a church strongly rooted in the Catholic middle class, sustained by their donations, staffed by their sons and daughters, and reflecting their moral and political prejudices and interests. This was to be demonstrated during the Lockout. The clergy in Dublin, with only a handful of exceptions, had always been hostile to the ITGWU, but hitherto they had limited themselves to sniping. Now they launched a full-scale assault that both the employers and the authorities hoped would prove decisive.

Clerical hostility had been in evidence since the ITGWU was founded, despite the Catholicism of the overwhelming majority of both its members and its leadership. Larkin, for example, was a practising Catholic, but one who had no intention of allowing any priest or bishop to interfere with either his politics or his union activity. He famously told a socialist meeting in the United States that there was "no antagonism between the cross and socialism" and that he stood by both the cross and Karl Marx: "Both *Capital* and the Bible are to me Holy Books".[66] Nevertheless, while the union would accept no clerical dictation, it made every effort to conciliate the church through the financial contributions of its members and by doing its best to avoid giving any offence over questions of morality. In this way, without any doubt, it reflected the sentiments of its members, but there certainly were occasions when it went too far in this regard. The priests were not impressed either. The *Irish Worker* reported stories of nuns telling children to refuse to go and buy the paper if sent for it by their parents and that priests were deliberately crossing picket lines at Fergusons the hairdressers during a bitter 12-week strike.

The sniping against the ITGWU was dramatically stepped up once the Lockout began. On a number of occasions the union was condemned from the pulpit by hostile priests. Larkin responded to these attacks with typical bluntness. He replied to an attack by Father John Condon by pointing out that in his sermon the Reverend Father had forgot to mention that he was "a shareholder in a commercial undertaking which is affected by the present deplorable dispute". Indeed, he went on to ask what Condon thought of "the 70-odd priests who are shareholders in the Dublin United Tramway Company and who are responsible, along with that other pillar of the church, William 'Murder' Murphy for the terrible bloodshed and tragedy of death".[67] The union responded to clerical attack with considerable vigour, retaliating with well-founded allegations of hypocrisy, accusing hostile priests of abandoning the poor for the service of Mammon.

Even given the level of clerical hostility, the church's intervention over the children's holiday scheme took the union by surprise. The scheme was modelled on the very successful children's holiday that had been organised by the IWW during the 1912 Lawrence strike in the US. The police intervened in Lawrence to prevent the children leaving the town, and their open brutality towards women and children had played an important part in winning public sympathy for the strikers. According to the IWW's historian, Melvyn Dubofsky, the Lawrence scheme "proved to be the strike's turning point".[68] The expectation was that the Dublin children's holiday would have the same effect, highlighting the way that the employers' strategy was dependent on starving the workers' children. The Dublin scheme was organised by Dora Montefiore, an experience socialist-feminist organiser and propagandist, in association with the *Daily Herald* and the Herald Leagues. Working class families in Britain came forward offering to put the Dublin children up and preparations were under way for the first group of children to go on holiday.

On 21 October 1913 the Archbishop of Dublin, William Walsh, publicly condemned the scheme for putting children at risk, both morally and pastorally. This provided an opportunity for the Hibernians and their clerical supporters to organise mobs to physically prevent the children from leaving the city. They were, it was claimed, being kidnapped and sent abroad to be proselytised or even sold into "white slavery". According to the Hibernian scab newspaper, the *Toiler*, the children were to be handed over to the Mormons and shipped to America.[69] Large mobs, led by priests, assembled at the railway stations to prevent children leaving and the police showed their traditional neutrality by allowing this intimidation and arresting the holiday scheme's organisers for kidnapping! Indeed, the police stood by while priests and Hibernians effectively took control of the stations and routinely held up and questioned any adults with children as to whether they were involved in the scheme.

Larkin responded defiantly, proclaiming that "I am not frightened by the archbishop or the priests... I say the priest who says I would allow a child to be proselytised is a liar in his heart. The religion that won't stand a month's holiday is not, by God, the religion I hold".[70] His involvement in the controversy ended on 28 October, however, when he was found guilty of sedition and sentenced to seven months in prison. While the union continued to defy clerical censure, it made clear that it would only place children in homes that had been approved by local priests. The offer was rejected. And even when the union attempted to send children to Irish Catholic homes in Belfast, this too was prevented by the Hibernians. It is absolutely clear that the whole furore was got up by the clergy to damage the union, and once they had the bit between their teeth, no union assurances were going to be acceptable. Writing in the *Daily Herald*, W P Ryan made the very pertinent point that the church had never objected when Irish youths, boys and girls, over many years had been sent to work at harvest time as farm labourers in Britain without any clerical supervision. There was no concern about morality then, only when it was a stick to beat the union.[71]

Archbishop Walsh gave the game away completely on 27 October when he urged people upset by "the sight of poor ill clad children" to "harden their hearts" and not give charity that would only prolong the dispute. As for the children's holiday scheme, he warned that it would only make the children "discontented with the poor homes to which they will sooner or later return, that is to say, those of them who return at all".[72] As George Russell sarcastically put it, the archbishop seemed perturbed by the prospect that if the children of the working class received proper meals in England, "they might be so inconsiderate as to ask for them all their lives".[73] The scheme was foiled, but the union successfully rode out the storm and the struggle continued. Larkin described the scheme as "the finest tactical error ever made", but took comfort from the fact that "the Dublin workers have withstood the shock of the priestly attack and now they know their friends".[74]

The ITGWU continued its defiance of clerical censure for the duration of the dispute. There were some overtures made to the clergy, but more in evidence was the *Irish Worker*'s condemnation of their refusal to help the poor. On 13 December 1913 James Stephens, the poet, published an article in the paper where he insisted that today "the difference between a priest and a policeman is too slight to talk about". The church's role in the Lockout was "cynical and disgusting". Later, after Archbishop Walsh congratulated the Home Rulers on their victory over the Labour Party in the local elections, in a front page article, the paper bitterly accused the clergy of "taking the side of greedy capitalist employers". "What remedy", the paper's columnist asked, "has any priest in the Archdiocese of Dublin, or in any Archdiocese or Diocese in Ireland attempted to find to remove the misery and wretchedness pressing so heavily and unjustly on the vast majority of the working classes? If they have made any attempt to find or to apply a remedy we plead ignorance of even having heard of such".[75] Even while adopting this defiant stand, the union still attempted to placate the church with regard to issues of morality, with Larkin on one occasion actually refusing to share a platform with a socialist divorcee in Grimsby!

On 13 June 1914, after the union had gone down to defeat, the *Irish Worker* carried an article, "The Sins of Capitalism: An Open Letter to Cardinal Logue", on its front page. Whereas Logue looked for reconciliation between capital and labour, the paper insisted that relations were "antagonistic, incompatible, irreconcilable and mutually destructive". There was a battle for "the conquest and control of economic power" between the capitalist class and the working class going on: "One or the other must go under, and we of the working class are determined it shall not be ourselves." The working class were fighting:

> until at last they control all industry, displacing employers, shattering wagery, profiteering, capitalism, and taking

to themselves the wealth they produce. The workers have a world to gain. And all the tinkering reform and dabbling in social science that the imagination of man can conjure up may delay, but will not prevent the march of the workers to the conquest of economic power. Your Eminence it means not reform but revolution... Your Eminence, society and capitalism have sinned against the working class. The working classes have sat in judgement upon the sinner, and in their good time and with their own chosen weapons shall the working classes exact the meet punishment. For the wages of sin is death.

Chapter 10

"Fiery Cross Crusade"

When Larkin was imprisoned on 28 October, the union and its supporters launched a campaign to secure his release. Connolly appealed to British workers to vote against the Liberal candidates in three pending by-elections in Reading, Keighley and Linlithgow. In all three by-elections socialists and trade unionists campaigned vigorously for the release of Larkin and the defeat of the Liberal candidate. The Liberals lost all three seats. The contrast between the treatment meted out to Larkin and the government's failure to take any action whatsoever against Sir Edward Carson and the Ulster Unionists was too obvious to be papered over. The Ulster Unionists were openly arming for civil war, with the full support of the Conservative Party, but it was on working men and women fighting for a better life that the full weight of the law came down! After only 17 days in prison Larkin was released. At a meeting at Liberty Hall on 13 December to celebrate what was a great victory, Larkin called for the campaign to continue to secure the release of the hundreds of other union members still in prison and promised to carry the fight across the water to Britain. He launched his "Fiery Cross Crusade". The Liberal government, he told his audience, had made a big mistake locking him up, but an even bigger one letting him out. At the same meeting Connolly announced the formation of a union militia, the Citizen Army.

While the battle over the children's holiday scheme raged, the employers had "brought in blacklegs under cover of the frenzy".[76] Interestingly enough, neither the Hibernians nor the clergy voiced any objection to this move on the part of the employers. The ITGWU, however, responded to the importation of hundreds of scabs by ordering an attempted return to mass picketing and by establishing the Citizen Army. By the end of November the Citizen Army had 1,200 members, many of them armed with iron shod pickaxe handles. They were to protect meetings and demonstrations, prevent police interference with picketing, fight the imported scabs, many of whom were provided with firearms by their employers, and prevent evictions. This last duty was particularly important during the winter of 1913-1914. As Richard Fox records, the Citizen Army was always:

> on the alert to prevent poor families being thrown into the streets because they couldn't pay their rent. When notice was given or action suspected, the Citizen Army men would rally and mount guard. On some occasions they carried sticks of furniture into houses from which tenants had been evicted.[77]

Armed scabs confronted the union with a real problem. They used their firearms freely and with complete impunity. On 29 November a scab shot a 50 year old woman, Bridget Rowe, in the face and walked free and on 18 December another scab shot 16 year old Alice Brady (she died from her wounds on 2 January) and once again escaped prosecution. Even when a scab accidentally shot and wounded one of the dock employers, Joseph Holloway, on 11 December, he walked free. By way of a contrast, union members were imprisoned for even calling a scab a scab. A union man was jailed for a year for throwing a policeman into the River Liffey—hardly a crime at all! Sometimes the workers had the better of it. On 18 January two armed scabs were overpowered by pickets who severely beat them both, killing one of them. The employers started a fund for the dead scab's dependents and Murphy, as a mark of his appreciation for someone dying to help preserve his wealth, donated a princely two guineas! This was, however, too unequal a battle. Imported scabs under heavy police protection were taking union members' jobs. If this went on the union was doomed to defeat. If the union was to win it needed solidarity action from workers in Britain. British unions had to black Dublin traffic.

Larkin launched his campaign for solidarity action, his "Fiery Cross Crusade", at the Free Trade Hall in Manchester on 16 November in front of a packed house of 4,000 with some 20,000 people turned away. He told his audience that he believed he had "a divine mission...to make men and women discontented". He was "out for revolution or nothing". British workers had "sent money and moral assistance" to Dublin, but now they had to help "get the scabs out of Dublin... We want to carry out the fundamentals and ethics of trade unionism, so don't scab on us. Are you going to allow us in Dublin to be offered up as a sacrifice?" In a swipe at the Catholic church, he told his audience that if William Martin Murphy was welcome in heaven, then he would rather go to hell. Hell "has no terrors for me. I have lived there." For many working class people life was hell and this was what they were fighting to change. He called on British workers "to stand by the men and women of Dublin till death". He laid into the leaders of the Labour Party, Ramsay Macdonald and Philip Snowden, for their refusal to support strikes, and castigated the leaders of the British trade unions for their refusal to win them.[78] Among the other speakers was the American IWW leader Big Bill Haywood, who had been on trade union business in France and had crossed the Channel to show solidarity (he brought with him a donation of 1,000 francs from the French trade union confederation, the CGT). Writing in the US journal, the *International Socialist Review*, Haywood described Larkin as "a fighter, every inch of him" and his speech ("And what a speech!") as "a terrific indictment". The war being waged against the Dublin workers was, Haywood told his American readers, "equalled only by some of the labour struggles that we have known so well in this country". Larkin "roused the audience at Manchester to a pitch of frenzy and a determination to stand by their Dublin brothers and sisters to the bitter end".[79]

Among the other speakers in Manchester was the dockers' leader, Ben Tillett. He called on British workers to arm, promised to lead them in battle against the police and to personally put an end to the home secretary, Reginald McKenna. Tillett was an old hand at socialist rhetoric, on one occasion telling a solidarity meeting in Bradford that the world was divided into thieves and slaves, and that the problem was that the thieves were very much aware that they were thieves but the slaves did not realise they were slaves.[80] At the very same time as he was prepared to talk socialism, preach revolution and pay lip service to solidarity, he was also doing his best to prevent any blacking of Dublin traffic on the docks. Tillett was a left official, who could talk the talk, but when it came to action he walked a different walk altogether. His dismal part in the struggle of the Dublin workers was not over.

On 19 November Larkin spoke at another massive meeting held at the Albert Hall in London under the auspices of the Herald Leagues. There was an audience of 12,000 with, once again, thousands turned away. On this occasion, an attempt was made by right wing students, "the sporting set", to disrupt the rally. They planned to turn off the lights and start a disturbance in the meeting, an "escapade" that would probably have had catastrophic consequences with people crushed in the ensuing panic. David Garnett, a student sympathetic to the Dublin workers, warned the organisers of what was planned and stewards prevented any interference with the lighting and threw out the handful of disrupters who managed to get in. To Garnett's horror, one of them was thrown bodily through a plate glass door although without suffering any serious injury. Outside the rally other members of "the sporting set" trying to force their way in clashed with the police with the result that the next morning "the Students Union was full of young men with bandaged heads". It is worth remembering that at this time university was very much the preserve of the children of the upper class and student loyalties reflected this. Garnett, incidentally, thought Larkin "the greatest orator I heard until Churchill...in June 1940".[81]

At the great Albert Hall rally Larkin once again attacked the Labour Party and the union leaders for their reluctance to fight, ridiculing them for their moderation and their continual attempts to placate the rich and powerful. But the TUC was at last being stirred to action. It was at the Albert Hall rally that the chairman announced to cheers that the TUC had called an unprecedented Special Conference to consider the situation in Dublin. These cheers then turned to jeers when he added that it would meet in three weeks on 9 December. Nevertheless, Larkin determined to seize the opportunity that this initiative seemed to provide. Once again Ben Tillett was on the platform alongside him preaching militancy, the need to meet force with force, and condemning those union leaders and Labour politicians who had no stomach for the fight.

According to Richard Fox, who was in the audience at the Albert Hall, the Fiery Cross Crusade, given:

> the prevailing militant mood of Labour, was bound to have repercussions. The older, more conservative leaders were troubled, especially as Larkin did not bother to conceal his contempt for them. "Penny plain and twopence coloured" was his description of the honoured but inactive leaders of Labour. He denounced them, jeered at them unmercifully and called to battle, while the eyes of young enthusiasts glowed and kindled.[82]

Larkin was seen as a dangerous, disruptive influence by the union bureaucracy. He was someone who was stirring up the rank and file and causing trouble. Fox recounts how even after the Dublin workers had been defeated, the rank and file in Britain still looked to Larkin for inspiration. Rank and file miners in Durham, where there was a strong syndicalist presence, secured an invitation for Larkin to speak at the Durham Miners' Gala in July 1914, much to the dismay of the full-time officials. They were "nervous about Larkin" and "made no effort to arrange for his coming". The platform was "crowded with portly, elderly men...a number of them had been Methodist preachers":

> The meeting had been going on for an hour or so when a roar of cheering was heard on the outskirts. The cheering grew louder and the vast crowd parted, leaving a laneway through which tramped a tall six-foot figure covered with dust and seething with anger. It was Larkin. He had walked miles from the nearest station to reach the meeting. The cheers were so deafening that the oratory ceased...he started his speech; a scathing, exultant tornado of a man, tumbling out all sorts of things which people felt but never said.[83]

During his Fiery Cross Crusade, Larkin spoke all over the country to packed meetings, calling for solidarity and for a labour movement that was ready to fight. At meeting after meeting he bitterly denounced those trade union and Labour Party leaders who refused to fight. This was, he insisted, a battle that could be won by working class solidarity. Victory for the Dublin workers was in the interest of all workers. If they won, it would inevitably strengthen the British labour movement; if they lost, the British labour movement would inevitably be weakened. And victory, he insisted, was within their grasp. In the words of one American socialist commentator, "Jim Larkin is here, there and everywhere." Indeed, by now, "his name spread terror throughout all Europe".[84]

Chapter 11

The rank and file act

The Fiery Cross Crusade was successful in provoking a second wave of unofficial action in support of the Dublin workers. Leading the way were Aslef members in South Wales, Driver James and Driver Reynolds, who were victimised for refusing to move "tainted" goods. Their sacking provoked an escalating strike that soon saw some 30,000 railwaymen, both Aslef and NUR members, out on strike. The union leaders moved decisively to suppress the action. The NUR leader, J H Thomas, a man who always had the employers' best interests at heart, forced through a return to work without securing the reinstatement of the two sacked drivers. Indeed, in order to bring Aslef members to heel, Thomas actually threatened to instruct NUR members to do their work. Thomas was, without doubt, one of the worst union leaders in British trade union history, a man whose overriding concern was to ingratiate himself with the employers and to whom selling his members out was second nature. He was, perhaps inevitably, to become a senior Labour Party politician, a member of Ramsay Macdonald's disastrous 1929-31 Labour government. When Macdonald defected to the Tories in 1931, Thomas went with him, a loyal servant of the ruling class right up until the end. Another of the Labour Party leaders whom Larkin routinely abused, Philip Snowden, was also to defect to the Tories at this time. During the Fiery Cross Crusade, Larkin had regularly warned his audiences to beware of those leaders "whom the capitalists patted on the back".[85]

Elsewhere on the docks full-time officials had their hands full, keeping their members at work and handling Dublin traffic. One London official complained that he had "never known a time when there has been manifested a desire to help any union in dispute as there is...towards their Dublin comrades". Officials had been abused by their members but, he reported, "so far we have been able to hold the men in check". He feared that if there were to be a strike, "it will be of such a magnitude as has never been equalled in any previous dispute".[86]

Instead of rallying to the support of the Dublin workers, who had always scrupulously blacked any tainted goods from Britain, British union leaders were instead determined to prevent any solidarity action. They did their best to reach an agreement with the Dublin Employers Federation over the head of the ITGWU and were only prevented from selling out the dispute by the intransigence of the employers. British union officials actually had a secret meeting with Archbishop Walsh at the height of the children's holiday scheme furore.[87] They were considerably more concerned with beating off a rank and file challenge to their own position, which they believed was inspired by Larkinism, than with helping the Dublin workers. Their modus operandi was to establish good relations with the employers by demonstrating their moderation and responsibility, and now here was Jim Larkin preaching discontent and revolt. He was a problem that they would have to deal with.

The Special TUC conference of 9 December was to be the decisive moment. On 22 November Larkin published a manifesto in the *Daily Herald*, condemning the moderation of the union leaders and urging the rank and file to force them to take action. "The British union leaders", he wrote, "seem to think, speak and act as though trade unionism was meant to be a salve for the sore of poverty," whereas "we say trade unionism is a root and branch remedy and by industrial action we can accomplish great things". He told the British working class that some of their leaders seemed to have forgotten the "fullest and highest spirit of trade union-ism...'An injury to one is an injury to all'." Too many union leaders seemed to "have forgotten that they once worked at the bench, in or out of the factory, on the docks or in the stokehole" and had instead become enamoured of "confer-ences, round tables, conciliation boards, and agreements". But men do "not live by agreements drawn up by the employ-ers' hirelings". Trade unionism was all about getting "the highest wages we can force from the employers" and "the best possible conditions". This required solidarity. Larkin urged his readers to pass resolutions and to send instructions so that the union leaders would have to "lead from the front and not from the rear, that they shall give voice to the rank and file". It had to be made clear "to those you have elected... that you, as organised workers, will no longer blackleg on your fellow workers". He insisted that:

> To blackleg is against the very basic principles of trade unionism. Therefore tell your leaders now and every day until December 9th, and raise your voices upon that date to tell them that they are not there as apologists for the short-comings of the capitalist system, that they are not there to assist the employers in helping to defeat any such section of workers striving to live, nor to act as a break on the wheel of progress. Tell them that this bloody warfare in Dublin must come to an end, this sacrifice of men, women and children must cease, and if they are not prepared to bring it to an end, then you of the rank and file will see to it that "finis" shall be written.

The manifesto is certainly a remarkable document that captures the essence of Larkinism. Nevertheless, in retro-spect, it was based on a tactical error. Larkin was urging the militants and activists who read the *Daily Herald* to make their leaders fight, to make them give a lead, to pass resolu-tions instructing them to black Dublin traffic. No amount of resolution passing on its own was going to make these men fight. It was not in their nature. What would have forced their hand was a widespread rank and file revolt involving the unofficial blacking of Dublin traffic. In these circumstances the leaders would have been obliged to make such action official in an attempt to take control of it.

Instead of calling for a deluge of resolutions and instructions in the run up to 9 December, Larkin should have been calling on the rank and file to take action before that date so as to force their hand. Why didn't he do this? As we have seen, there was considerable unrest on the docks and the railways, unrest that could have caught fire. Instead Larkin seems to have put his faith in left wing union leaders, in the hope that the likes of Ben Tillett would carry the day and that 9 December would see an unprecedented vote in favour of solidarity action.

Some of Larkin's critics, both at the time and today, argue that his attacks on the union and Labour Party leaders were a serious mistake because they needlessly alienated these men and turned them against the cause of the Dublin workers. There are two things wrong with this criticism: first it mistakes the temper of the times. This was a period of great rank and file revolt. The ITGWU itself was a product of this revolt and Larkin was its spokesman, not just in Ireland but throughout Britain as well. This revolt was a rank and file response to the refusal of the union leaders to fight. It involved a recognition on the part of masses of union members of the conservatism of the full-time officials, of the fact that if they wanted action it would have to be unofficial and directed as much against the union bureaucracy as against the employers. This was the pattern in strike after strike throughout the period of the Great Unrest. And, of course, a good case can be made that Larkin had a much more accurate understanding of the character of the leaders of the British labour movement. If he had been polite, respectful, even flattering, to the likes of Thomas and Macdonald, Snowden and Havelock Wilson, this would have made no difference whatsoever to their determination not to fight. Persuasion and argument would not work with these people. The only hope of solidarity action in support of the Dublin workers was through unofficial blacking and rank and file pressure. Larkin's mistake was that he put too much faith in those officials who talked left, not recognising that in the end for too many of them their loyalty was to trade union officialdom rather than the rank and file.

Chapter 12

Betrayal

There is an old joke that if the TUC had been in existence at the time of the Tolpuddle Martyrs in the 1830s and had taken charge of their defence campaign then they would still be in exile in Tasmania today. Such lack of confidence in the effectiveness of the TUC when it comes to winning disputes was completely borne out by the 9 December conference. What Larkin and Connolly found themselves confronted with on that fateful day was not a conference of delegates mandated by the rank and file, but a conference completely dominated by full-time officials.

According to Bill Moran, there was not one delegate who had been formally elected or mandated for the conference; instead they were all either appointed by their union executives or chosen from among the delegates to the annual TUC.[88] Even worse, there were bona fide trade unionist delegates known to be sympathetic to Larkin denied accreditation, while Labour Party and Fabian Society representatives were allowed in and allowed to vote. Indeed, one of them, W C Anderson, who was not even a member of a trade union, actually seconded the motion censuring Larkin! As Richard Fox succinctly put it, while the conference was supposedly "to decide what was to be done about Dublin", in fact, "it was to decide what was to be done about Larkin".[89] Indeed, many of the union leaders assembled there, the likes of J H Thomas, Havelock Wilson of the seamen and Larkin's old adversary, James Sexton of the NUDL, were actually more worried by the prospect of the Dublin workers winning than they were by the prospect of the ITGWU being destroyed. A victory for the Dublin workers would be a victory for Larkinism that would inspire their own rank and file members to unwelcome militancy. They and the employers had a shared interest in the defeat of the ITGWU.

What took Larkin completely by surprise, however, was the ownership of the hand that struck the fatal blow. The resolution put to the conference censoring Larkin for his attacks on the British trade union leadership was proposed by none other than Ben Tillett. The knife was plunged into the ITGWU's back by a man who had stood on the platform alongside Larkin when he had been abusing the likes of Thomas; indeed, Tillett had actually joined in the abuse! Tillett's moving the resolution opened the floodgates for attack after attack on Larkin, and the censure vote was carried almost unanimously with only six delegates voting against out of some 600.

On the question of how to help the Dublin workers, Larkin vigorously rejected any attempt to settle the dispute over the heads of the ITGWU membership. He welcomed the TUC's financial help, but insisted that, while useful, "money never won a strike". Solidarity won strikes. The dispute would be won if only the British trade unions would refuse to handle goods loaded by scabs and black Dublin traffic: "all they had to say was that Dublin was a self-contained town".[90] The proposal to black Dublin traffic was defeated by an overwhelming 2,280,000 votes to 203,000.

This was a crushing setback, all the more so as it was Larkin's belief that many Dublin employers were themselves exhausted by the struggle and that even the threat of British trade union solidarity would have broken up the Dublin Employers Federation with many of them rushing to settle on the union's terms. He believed quite correctly that victory was within their grasp. Instead the TUC had thrown the Dublin employers a lifeline and left the Dublin workers to be defeated.[91] What of Ben Tillett? He subsequently gave up any pretence of radicalism, moved to the right and with grim inevitability became a Labour MP in 1917. He was a strong supporter of the First World War and remained in the Commons until 1931. On at least one occasion while a Labour MP, he privately approached the Conservative Party for money![92]

Connolly summed the situation up when he wrote in the Glasgow *Forward* of how "[we asked] that the working class of Britain should help us to prevent the Dublin capitalists carrying on their business without us. We asked for the isolation of the capitalists of Dublin, and for answer the leaders of the British labour movement proceeded calmly to isolate the working class of Dublin". Instead of receiving "the sacramental wafer of brotherhood and common sacrifice", the Dublin workers had to "eat the dust of defeat and betrayal".[93]

Chapter 13

Defeat

The TUC's betrayal made defeat inevitable. The only question in Dublin now was what terms could be secured for a return to work. On 16 December the union secretly advised its members to settle where possible, but for the great majority the struggle continued over the Christmas period and into the new year. The larger employers continued to import scabs from Britain and violent street clashes continued as the union battled to drive them out. With men beginning to return to work, the ITGWU leadership recognised that there was no hope of victory and instead decided to save what it could. On 18 January the union ordered a return to work where possible. There were still some hard fought battles and it was not until the middle of March that the workers at Jacob's, overwhelmingly women workers, finally gave in and returned on their employers' terms. There was widespread victimisation with many workers sacked and blacklisted. At Jacob's hundreds lost their jobs. Many firms withdrew union recognition, although few actually tried to enforce the document. Murphy was, of course, an exception. But the ITGWU survived, maintaining its position on the docks.

In an editorial that appeared in the *Irish Worker* on 7 February 1914 Larkin, battered but unbowed, assessed the situation. William "Murder" Murphy's victory celebrations were ill judged. The union had taken on "all the forces of reaction combined; priests, press, publicans, police, plutocrats—all of whom are but sections of the capitalist forces, backed up by a government that will go down in history as the disgrace of the century". But, he insisted, the union had them beat: "We would have driven all these various forces in on themselves if it had not been for the foul, insidious conspiracy, based on personal vindictiveness of the alleged British Labour leaders and their action in advising sections under their control to sell their honour and their class." For the time being, the union had been forced to "retire to our base", but plans were being prepared "for another advance". He went on:

> What of the new campaign, constructive and yet destructive, the ideal that we set forth in our salad days is still our ideal; a co-operative Commonwealth... We appeal to our readers to enter into our work with the spirit that animates us. There can be great things accomplished by united effort... Surely the women and men who have endured for six months the arrows of outrageous fortune and envenomed devilment of the Dublin employing class and their paid hirelings, are too good a metal to flux in the melting pot of capitalist exploitation. No friend, not Murphyism, by the rank rotter; but the Labourism of the Wilson-Thomas-Sexton type, the political expediency of the Macdonald-Snowden type, the foulness and treachery of our own class gave us pause, and as like the runner, we are getting our second breath, and then we will make the pace a hot one.

Conclusion

Recovery from defeat in 1913-14 took longer than Larkin envisaged. The ITGWU was to throw itself into opposition to the First World War, but Larkin himself was to leave on a fundraising visit to America in October 1914, not to return to Ireland until the end of April 1923, deported, after a term in Sing Sing prison, for his Communist beliefs. In the spring of 1916 a reorganised Citizen Army, led by Jim Connolly, was to play a crucial role in the Easter Rising. Connolly was among those executed by British firing squad in the aftermath. But it was in the years from 1917 through to 1923 that there was a second great wave of working class revolt in Ireland, more widespread and more protracted than the earlier Larkinite offensive. This second wave saw strikes, general strikes and factory occupations before it was over. Whereas in 1917 the ITGWU had only 14,000 members, by 1920 the number had increased dramatically to 120,000. Irish trade unions were to play an important part in the War of Independence. This, however, is another story.[94]

Today we are in the middle of the most sustained attack on the working class since the 1930s, not just in Britain and Ireland, but across Europe, in the United States and much of the rest of the world. The capitalist class internationally is driving down living standards, dismantling welfare provision and attacking working class organisation in an unprecedented way. This attack has only just begun and yet already it has wreaked tremendous damage, inflicting misery and hardship on millions of people. Divide and rule is the name of the game. The cost of the economic crisis is to be paid by the working class with the rich and super-rich increasing their wealth and power while the rest of us suffer cut after cut. In the face of this attack, the union leaders and the leaders of the Labour and Socialist parties throughout the West seem to have decided, in the main, to sit on their hands. This is a recipe for disaster and must be fought. The tide has to be turned.

What can we learn from the experience of the Dublin working class and their British supporters and sympathisers during the Great Lockout? The key lesson is the importance of solidarity. The capitalist class prospers by divide and rule. This has to be met with working class solidarity. The Dublin workers achieved great things at home by solidarity and, as we have seen, routinely supported the struggles of British workers. When they were locked out and facing a concerted attack involving the employers, police and troops, the press, the clergy, the courts, the Home Rule party and the Liberal government, the British trade union leadership, urged on by the leaders of the Labour Party, not only refused to take solidarity action, but set about stamping it out when the rank and file took action unofficially. The Dublin Lockout could and should have been won, but the British trade union bureaucrats saw Larkin as a bigger threat to their position than the employers were. In the end Larkin and Larkinism had to be curbed and the Dublin workers were left to go down to defeat. The need for rank and file organisation and for socialist politics was crucial in 1913 and it remains crucial today.

Notes

1 The *Daily Herald* was sold to Rupert Murdoch in 1969. It had already changed its name to the *Sun*, but under Murdoch it became a right wing, xenophobic, anti trade union paper that enthusiastically encouraged scabbing, established new standards of dishonesty and character assassination, engaged in systematic criminality over many years and has had more of its executives and journalists arrested by the police than any other newspaper in British history. See my "'Most Humble Day': the Murdoch Empire on the Defensive", *International Socialism* 134 (spring 2012).

2 See the discussion in my *Rebel City: Larkin, Connolly and the Dublin Labour Movement* (London, 2004), pp10-11.

3 The ITGWU was not the only breakaway from the NUDL. Larkin's suspension, the example of the ITGWU and Sexton's authoritarianism were factors in the establishment of the Scottish Union of Dock Labourers in Glasgow that succeeded in organising the Glasgow docks in 1911-12. See William Kenewick, *'Rebellious and Contrary': The Glasgow Dockers 1853-1932* (East Lothian, 2000), pp200-212.

4 Francis Devine, *Organising History: A Centenary of SIPTU* (Dublin, 2009), p24.

5 Bob Holton, *British Syndicalism 1900-1914* (London, 1976), p73.

6 Holton, as above, p89.

7 *Irish Worker*, 19 August 1911.

8 Emmet Larkin, *James Larkin* (London, 1968), p83.

9 *Irish Worker*, 4 May 1912.

10 *Irish Worker*, 4 January 1913.

11 Devine, as above, p46.

12 Larkin, as above, p103.

13 Joseph O'Brien, *"Dear Dirty Dublin": A City in Distress 1899-1916* (Berkeley, 1982), p223.

14 See Newsinger, *Rebel City*, as above, pp40-42.

15 Holton, as above, pp207-208.

16 R M Fox, *Jim Larkin: The Rise of the Underman* (London, 1957), pp107-108, 110.

17 Larkin, as above, p69.

18 Robert Lowery, "Sean O'Casey and the *Irish Worker*" in Robert Lowery (ed), *O'Casey Annual* no 3 (London, 1984), pp42-43. See also my "'In the Hunger-cry of the Nation's Poor is Heard the Voice of Ireland': Sean O'Casey and Politics", *Journal of Contemporary History* 20, 3 (1985) and my "Sean O'Casey, Larkinism and Literature", *Irish Studies Review*, 12, 3 (2004).

19 C Desmond Greaves, *The Irish Transport and General Workers Union: The Formative Years* (Dublin, 1982), p58.

20 Fox, as above, p74.

21 For Wilson see Steven Dedalus Burch, *Andrew P Wilson and the Early Irish and Scottish National Theatres 1911-1950* (Lampeter, 2008).

22 W P Ryan, *The Irish Labour Movement* (Dublin, 1919),

p181. At the time of the Great Lockout, Ryan was deputy editor of the *Daily Herald* and a staunch supporter of the ITGWU.

23 *Irish Worker*, 26 July 1913.

24 *Irish Worker*, 2 August 1913.

25 *Irish Worker*, 22 February 1913.

26 For Kavanagh see James Curry, *Artist of the Revolution: The Cartoons of Ernest Kavanagh* (Cork, 2012).

27 *Irish Worker*, 15 July 1911.

28 *Irish Worker*, 27 July 1912.

29 The Ancient Order of Hibernians was a Catholic sectarian organisation, the equivalent of the Protestant Orange Order. It had close links with the Home Rule party and was often used to do the party leadership's dirty work.

30 *Irish Worker*, 21 March 1914.

31 *Irish Worker*, 23 November 1912.

32 *Irish Worker*, 4 January 1913.

33 For the 1790s see my *United Irishman: The Autobiography of James Hope* (London, 2001) and for 1848 and the 1860s see my *Fenianism in Mid-Victorian Britain* (London, 1994).

34 *Irish Worker*, 26 April 1913.

35 See Bill McCamley, *Dublin's Tramworkers 1872-1945* (Dublin, 2008), pp56-59.

36 *Freeman's Journal*, 22 August 1913.

37 Padraig Yeates, *Lockout: Dublin 1913* (Dublin, 2000), p49. Yeates provides what is by far the best account of the police assault over these days and nights in his epic account of the Lockout, an account that has not yet been surpassed.

38 Jim Phelan, *The Name's Phelan* (London, 1948), p151.

39 For the forgotten death of 68 year old James Carey at the hands of the police see Yeates, as above, pp270-271.

40 Dermot Keogh, *The Rise of the Dublin Working Class* (Belfast, 1982), p202.

41 On a number of occasions over this bloody weekend troops were called out to reinforce the police and there were reports of "the protest of the 5th Lancers" about this strikebreaking and that the men of the West Kent Regiment were only "very reluctantly" guarding the trams. This was, "of course, hushed up". See *Justice*, 13 September 1913.

42 Phelan, as above, p154.

43 Fox, as above, p88.

44 James Connolly, "Glorious Dublin", *Forward*, 4 October 1913. *Forward* was a Glasgow socialist newspaper that Connolly wrote for regularly.

45 See my *Rebel City*, as above, p60.

46 *Justice*, 22 November 1913.

47 Yeates, as above, p374.

48 *Justice*, 6 September 1913.

49 *Forward*, 4 October 1913.

50 See my *Rebel City*, as above, p54.

51 *Freeman's Journal*, 2 September 1913.

52 Fox, as above, p98.

53 Fox, as above, p100.

54 Hugh Geraghty, *William Patrick Partridge* (Dublin, 2003), p201.

55 Harry Gosling, *Up and Down Stream* (London, 1927), pp120-123.

56 R M Fox, *Smoky Crusade* (London, 1937), p150.

57 See Eric Taplin, *Near To Revolution: The Liverpool General Transport Strike 1911* (Liverpool, 1994).

58 Martin Crick, *The History of the Social Democratic Federation* (Keele, 1994), pp246, 249. According to Crick, the BSP's paid-up membership was more like 13,000. The BSP was to split during the First World War with its best elements helping to establish the Communist Party of Great Britain in 1920.

59 *Justice*, 13 September 1913. See my unpublished paper, "'The duty of Social Democrats in this Labour Unrest': Justice and the Dublin Lockout".

60 *Justice*, 29 November 1913.

61 Gosling, as above, pp125-126.

62 Percy Redfern, *The New History of the CWS* (London, 1938), p81. See also Theresa Moriarty, "'Who Will Look After The Kiddies?': Households and Collective Action During The Dublin Lockout, 1913", in Jan Kok (ed), *Rebellious Families* (New York, 2002). The relief effort was enormous. As Moriarty reveals, every morning the union provided breakfast for 3,000 children.

63 See my *Rebel City*, as above, pp90-91.

64 Harry McShane, *No Mean Fighter* (London, 1978), pp57-58.

65 *Forward*, 9 February 1914.

66 See my *Rebel City*, as above, pp32-37.

67 *Irish Worker*, 20 September 1913.

68 Melvyn Dubofsky, *We Shall Be All: A History of the Industrial Workers of the World* (Urbana, 2000), pp146-147.

69 For the *Toiler* see my "'The Curse of Larkinism': Patrick McIntyre, *The Toiler* and the Dublin Lockout of 1913", *Eire-Ireland*, vol XXX, no 3 (1995).

70 Larkin, as above, p125.

71 *Daily Herald*, 23 October 1913.

72 See my *Rebel City*, as above, p74.

73 John Newsinger, "Reporting the 1913 Lockout: the Freeman's Journal, Larkinism and the Dublin Labour Troubles", *Saothar* 28 (2003), p131.

74 *Daily Herald*, 28 October 1913.

75 *Irish Worker*, 24 January 1914.

76 Devine, as above, p60.

77 Fox, *Jim Larkin*, as above, p117.

78 *Freeman's Journal*, 17 November 1913.

79 William D Haywood, "Larkin's Call for Solidarity", *International Socialist Review*, February 1914, p470. That same issue of the *Review* gives a real feel of the ferocity of the class struggle in the US at this time with reports on the murderous miners' strikes in Calumet, Michigan and in Colorado, soon to be the scene of the Ludlow massacre.

80 *Justice*, 29 November 1913.

81 David Garnett, *The Golden Echo* (London, 1953), pp203-206.

82 Fox, *Smoky Crusade*, as above, p168.

83 Fox, *Jim Larkin*, as above, pp110-111.

84 Caroline Nelson, "Jim Larkin", *International Socialist Review*, December 1913, p335.

85 *Freeman's Journal*, 1 December 1913.

86 See my *Rebel City*, as above, p94.

87 Yeates, as above, p287.

88 Bill Moran, "1913, Jim Larkin and the British Labour Movement", *Saothar* 4 (1978), p44.

89 Fox, *Smoky Crusade*, as above, p172.

90 *Freeman's Journal*, 10 December 1913.

91 What was the response of the BSP to the 9 December conference? In the pages of *Justice* (13 December 1913) the party supported the motion of censure on Larkin, although it regretted that it had been first on the agenda, and while it also supported the motion to black Dublin traffic, it had no explanation for the overwhelming defeat of the proposal. Indeed, all it had to say was that "it would have been better had it not been held". There was no discussion of the politics of the affair or of the way forward at all. Its main concern was to attack syndicalism and the *Daily Herald*. The party leadership was committed to its members becoming part of the trade union bureaucracy, rather than supporting any rank and file challenge.

92 Jonathan Schneer, *Ben Tillett* (Beckenham, 1982), pp218-219.

93 *Forward*, 9 February 1914.

94 See my *Rebel City*, as above, pp156-174. See also Conor Kostick, *Revolution in Ireland* (London, 2009), a superb account of these years.